IMAGES
of America

SAGAMORE
BEACH

Original houses on the Bluff at Sagamore Beach are shown c. 1910 with the new form of transportation in the foreground. (Photograph by Henry Dickerman and Son for Adams Pharmacy, courtesy of Town of Sandwich Archives.)

IMAGES
of America

SAGAMORE
BEACH

Marion R. Vuilleumier

ARCADIA
PUBLISHING

Published by Arcadia Publishing
Charleston, South Carolina

Library of Congress Catalog Card Number: 2003101267

For all general information, contact Arcadia Publishing:
Telephone 843-853-2070
Fax 843-853-0044
E-mail sales@arcadiapublishing.com
For customer service and orders:
Toll-Free 1-888-313-2665

Visit us on the Internet at www.arcadiapublishing.com

Assembly Hall, designed by Oscar Thayer, was built in 1907 on Robinson Road. It was created for the Christian Endeavor movement as a religious center of the community.

CONTENTS

ACKNOWLEDGMENTS

Heartfelt appreciation is expressed to Barbara Doran Sullivan, who has worked ceaselessly to locate images for this book. Sincere thanks also go to the many people from the Sagamore Beach community who shared their personal family photographs: Patricia Amirault, Nancy Anderson, Ben Arnold, Malcolm Banks, Ann Decaneas, Peggy Ann Dolan, Eleanor Doran, Rachel Fagerburg, Champe Fisher, Clark Fisher, Frederick G. Fisher III, Patricia Flanagan, Norman Hill, Jeannine Holway, Jackie Jacobson, Drew Knowland, Arthur LaCroix, Polly and Joe Leis, Richard and Cynthia Locke, Debbie McCahill, Jim Newell, Beverly Niit, Sue Newell Reilly, Jennifer Sorenti, Barbara Thibault, Mary Jane Tuohy, Audrey Werthen, and the Zickell family.

In addition, special thanks go to Barbara Gill, archivist for the Sandwich Archives and Historical Center; Nezka Pfeifer, curator at the Sandwich Glass Museum; Barbara Condon of the Bourne Historical Center and Archives; and Mary Sicchio, special collections librarian at Cape Cod Community College. Sincere thanks go to Barnstable historian James Gould for early map information and to Sandwich historian Russell A. Lovell Jr., author of *Sandwich: A Cape Cod Town*, which contains a wealth of information about the upper Cape.

Off on a boat trip *c.* 1967 are, from left to right, the following: (front row) Ellen Flanagan, Tricia Sullivan, Susie Flanagan, Ted Dolan, and Maureen Flanagan; (back row) Debbie Dolan, Michael Flanagan, and Diane Dolan.

INTRODUCTION

Although Sagamore Beach today is a vibrant village in Cape Cod's newest town, human life began here in the mists of history. Long before white-skinned people arrived, Wampanoag Indians roamed the woods and fields. In 1637, this area became part of the first permanent settlement of Sandwich. Simeon Deyo, author of the 1890 *History of Barnstable County*, noted on a map some of the Native American tribes in the general area: Scusset, Manamet, Shaume, and Patuxet (whose people were to the north in what is today's Plymouth). These tribes were mobile, staying near the shore in summer and inland in winter. They had created an important trail that went east to the outer Cape. This trail was used by the white settlers, who widened it, and it was to become the only artery of land traffic for the next 200 years. It crossed the swampy land of Scusset Creek over the Indian Stepping Stones and later traversed a causeway. Eventually, the trail became the basis for the King's Highway and then, with modifications, today's Route 6A.

At first, there were only a few fishermen's cottages and an occasional farmhouse along the path between the Plymouth line and the Scusset causeway. The area was then known as Sandwich's West Sagamore. There were two small hamlets: Sagamore Beach and Sagamore Highlands. In 1884, when the dredging of the planned Cape Cod Canal began, which was to make Cape Cod an island, Bourne was divided from Sandwich. Thus the community in Sagamore Beach, a village in the Cape's oldest town, became a village in the Cape's newest town.

It was not until 1905 that the population of Sagamore Beach suddenly burgeoned, when it was settled by members of the Christian Endeavor Society. Impressed by the pristine beach and its background of dunes, cliffs, and wooded land, members found it ideal for a combined vacation, recreational, and religious community. The Sagamore Beach Company was formed, property surveyed, and lots laid out. Sales were brisk, and soon cottages and two inns had been built. The creation of the Sagamore Beach Colony Club in 1909 gave impetus to a variety of programs. Speakers of national fame were corralled, no doubt with the help of residents Dr. Francis E. Clark, president of the Christian Endeavor movement, and Prof. Amos Wells, longtime editor of the *Christian Endeavor World*. Talks were given first under a large tent and, by 1907, in Assembly Hall. Sagamore Beach soon became internationally known as a religious center, featuring Christian Endeavor institutes, Sunday school conferences, and meetings of Friends (Quakers). Sports and family activities were always featured at these gatherings, especially the traditional daily 11:00 a.m. swim.

Life in the colony settled into a routine, with morning and evening mail delivered at the temporary post office; water sports, tennis, and other games taking place at the Playstead; and, of course, religious services being conducted. Before the days of automobiles, colonists could walk to Scusset Creek's outlet to buy fish at a local fish house, to Sagamore for movies and a soda, or to Lake Manomet, where residents could enjoy overnight camping and freshwater swimming. Among the adult programs offered were a reading circle, basket-making and watercolor classes, and play readings. Annual dramas were presented in the Dell, a natural amphitheater. Programs featured Pilgrim and patriot themes, with an occasional Shakespeare play.

The two biggest summer events were on the Fourth of July and at Colony Day. A town crier woke everyone with his bell. Water and land sports followed. Early in the afternoon, the cottages held open house with hostesses serving refreshments. Then, everyone paraded to the Dell in costume to enjoy the drama presented by residents.

Meanwhile, residents could not escape noticing events outside the colony. People had a good view of the building of the jetties for the Cape Cod Canal. The beach jetties were in fact a blessing to the community, for they stopped the erosion of the Bluff. Residents had a front-row view of the dredging, the building of the first bridge over the old causeway, the erection of the Sagamore Bridge in the 1930s, and the first ships in transit on the canal. Early residents, who arrived by train in Sagamore and then traveled by horse and buggy to the beach, watched with interest the arrival of the automobiles and the laying of the trolley track from Plymouth (which very few trolleys saw), and they heard the droning of aircraft overhead. Electricity, the telephone, and the radio made life easier.

Much ado was made about the 50th anniversary of the Sagamore Beach Colony, celebrated in 1955, and the 75th anniversary in 1980. Sidney Clark, noted travel writer and son of Dr. Francis E. Clark, chronicled the first anniversary. He wrote most of his famed travel books at his beach cottage. Other well-known residents were Joseph W. Martin, Speaker of the House of Representatives, and Mabel Batchelder of the National Republican Committee.

Officers of the colony realized early the importance of zoning as an aid in keeping the community residential and upholding its emphasis on family and religious activities. Thus, the commercial part of the village is clustered around the Sagamore Bridge, and the rest remains a quiet residential area with the exception of the Little Store. The town clerk reports that there are now 3,337 year-round residents, but the population burgeons to about 6,600 in summer. According to the *Cape Cod Times*, "the best thing about Sagamore Beach is that it has no profile." People tend to drive right by it, so it remains somewhat hidden. It is also a good example of how a summer colony can gradually segue into a vibrant year-round community that still keeps to its original purpose.

One

THE BEGINNING

For many thousands of years before the English settled in southeastern Massachusetts, the land was populated by Native Americans. In this area, they were from the Algonquin group, part of the eastern woodland culture, according to Leo Bonfanti in his book *New England Indians*. When the Pilgrims arrived in Plimoth (later Plymouth) in 1620, there were about 30 Native American tribes in what is now southeastern Massachusetts and eastern Rhode Island, known as the Wampanoag Indian Federation. Massasoit was their Supreme Sachem, and after an uneasy period when messages passed back and forth, the Pilgrims and the Wampanoags met and signed a treaty.

Like all of the Cape Cod area, today's Sagamore Beach section was once heavily forested. There was a Native American trail that went through it, used by the Wampanoags to reach the sea and the territory of the Nauset tribe. In other respects, the scenery remained almost unchanged until 1637. At that time, 10 men and their families arrived from Saugus to settle along the borders and streams on the shore overlooking Cape Cod Bay. The Sandwich territory then extended from the Plimoth line to the Barnstable town line, with the center about where Scusset River entered the bay. Both Barnstable and Yarmouth were settled in 1639, thus increasing travel on the Native American trail. The settlers had soon widened the trail (called Colonial Road on some early maps) as travel increased between Plimoth and the Cape towns.

Historian Russell A Lovell Jr. notes that there were 60 families settled in Sandwich by 1637, and despite many changes, "the initial population factors remained almost in balance to 1650." By 1883, the population had increased to 3,544. There had been several attempts to divide the town, one in consideration of the distance that people had to travel to the Sandwich Town Hall. Another reason for wanting to divide the town was the imminent prospect of a canal that would have to be cut through Sandwich, since it had the narrowest neck of land that separated Cape Cod from the mainland. Native Americans, and later the Pilgrims, had portaged goods the short distance from Scusset River headquarters south to Manamet River and down to the southern bay.

Lovell notes that when the question of town division arose in 1884, senators and representatives came by train from Boston to Cataumet to view the situation. It was a rainy day when they boarded a line of carriages with local hosts, to go up the main road through the villages over muddy tracks. "When the exhausted committees got to Central House in Sandwich four hours later, they were told by David Nye that was the way he had to go at least once a week for selectmen's meetings!" On a later visit, political representatives were given a tour of the glass factory and a view of a dredge already working at the canal site. A unanimous decision was made to divide the town. The vote passed in the House of Representatives with a majority of 23, and when the act was signed by the governor on April 2, 1884, the Cape's 15th town, Bourne, came into being. The residents of Sagamore Beach next paid their taxes in Bourne.

Although taken long after Sagamore Beach was colonized, this photograph shows a view that could well be similar to what the early settlers saw when they looked north toward the Highlands. (Courtesy of Sandwich Glass Museum.)

This map of the Plimoth Colony was drawn by Channing Howard in 1937. It shows the Native American settlements at the time of the arrival of the white men. (Courtesy of Bourne Historical Society.)

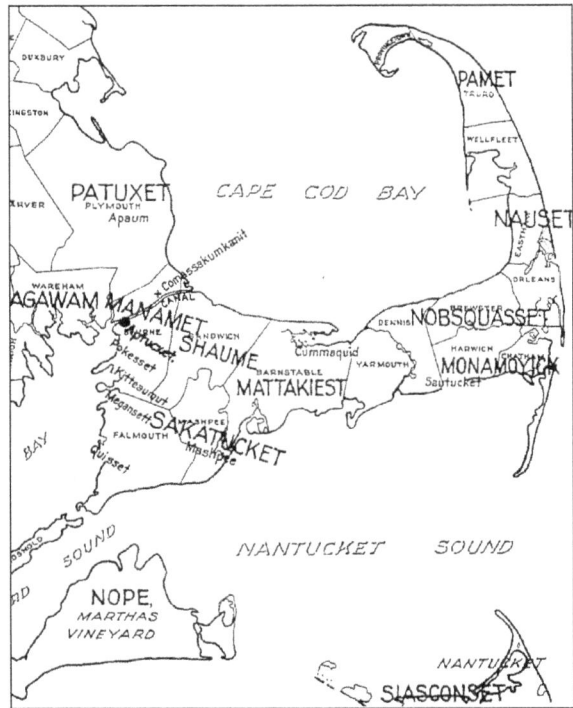

This Wampanoag Indian sharpening rock was one of those used as community grinding stones. A prime example, it was found at the end of the trail in Nauset Indian tribe territory. Today it can be seen in Eastham, where it lies under a protective shelter in the Cape Cod National Seashore Park, at the approximate eastern end of the trail. The broad channels in the rock were used to sharpen stone axes. Its nearly flat surfaces were used to grind cutting edges of tomahawks and chisels, and its narrow grooves were used to shape fishhooks made of bone. (Sketch by Louis Vuilleumier.)

11

PEAKED CLIFF

John Ellis

to Plymouth

SANDWICH

SAGAMORE HIGHLANDS

Thomas Butler

CAPE

SCUSS

BASS CREEK

(INDIAN TRAIL/COLONIAL ROAD)

Thomas Gibbs

SAG

NORTH SAGAMORE

William Swift

KEY

🏠 Approximate location of house in 1657 (most go back to 1637)

🏠 Grist Mill

Q Quaker

[ ] Modern feature

☀ Upland

✹ Marsh

Adapted from maps of Russell A. Lovell, Jr.

𝕾 Spring

↓ BOUNDARY TO ROCK AT HERRING POND

J. W. Gould 15 III 1997

N

Michael Blackwell

Indian Stepping Stones

SCUSSET CREEK

[Sagamore Bridge 1935]

Indian Portage to Manomet River ½ mile, to Aptuxet, Herring Pond

Fr

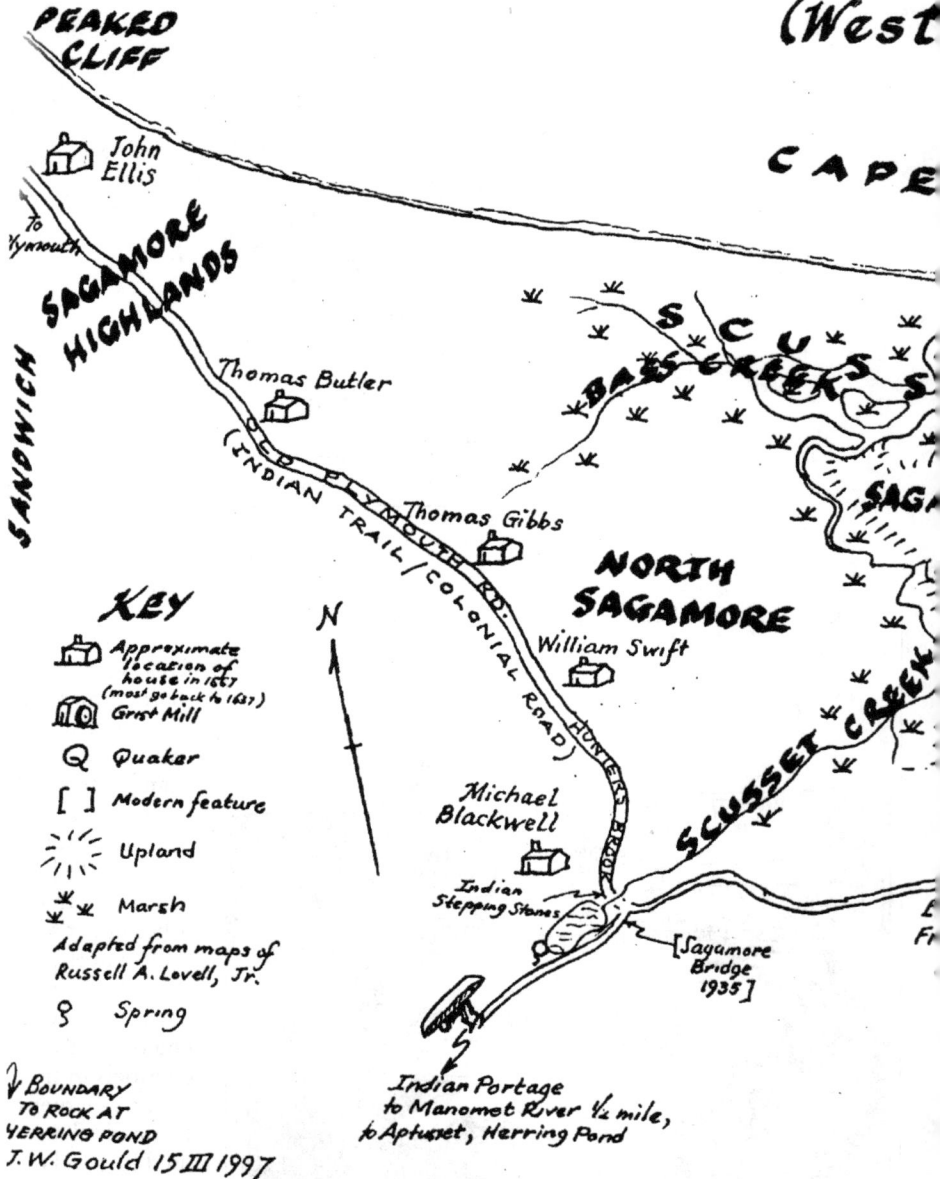

This map, showing the probable location of the original Native American trail from Plymouth to the Nauset area of the outer Cape, was drawn by Barnstable historian James Gould of Cotuit, in cooperation with Sandwich historian Russell A. Lovell Jr. The map was first published by the Cape Cod Genealogical Society in the 1997 spring-summer issue of its journal.

BAY

HARBOR

MARSH

TOWN
NECK
(CALF PASTURE)

SHAWME RIVER

SHAWME

HARBOR

John
Jenkins

John
Ellisfish

Richard
Bourne

Town Dock

Thomas Tupper Sr.

John
Fish

John
Chipman
1654

Samuel
Briggs

Joseph
Burgess

FORD
SWAMP

THE LOTS:

First
Bridge

First
leverinch

Rev.

James
Skiff

CHARLES

Peter Gaunt
Q

Church
1694

cardinal

Michael Turner
Q

Dexter
Mill
1638

MAIN ST.

UPPER

Francis Allen

Lower Rd.

George Knott

William
Bassett

le E.
Graves

Thomas
Tupper Jr.

Camp Ground
Rd.

Rev. John
Smith
1675

Browabread
Hill

CROSS ST.

William
Newland
Q

SHAWME POND

Daniel
Wing
Q

[R.T. 130]

George
Built

Thomas Tobey

Back St.

Upper
Pond
(Marsh)

Edward
Dillingham

To
Mashpee

To Pocasset

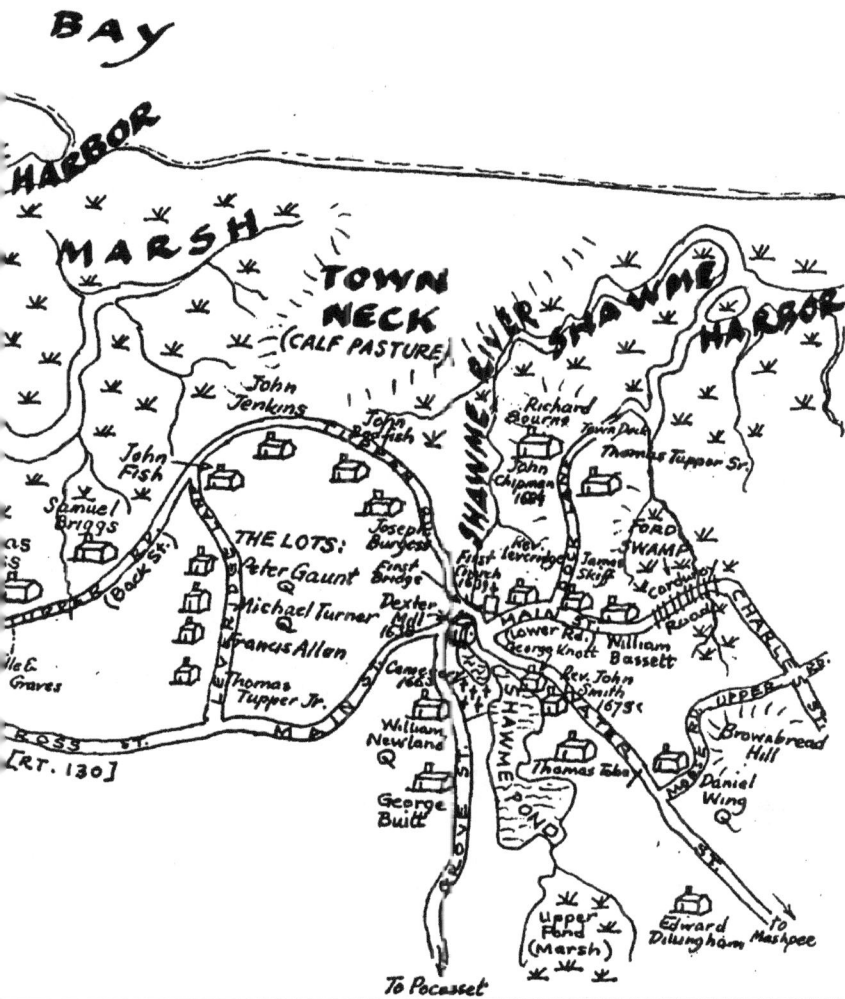

Gould noted that the Wampanoags crossed the rivers and brooks inland in order to have less water area to cross. Note the location of the Indian Stepping Stones, which were quite close to the placement of today's Sagamore Bridge. (Courtesy of James Gould and Cape Cod Community College Archives.)

Rev. Edmund E. Phillips of Sagamore is shown drinking water from the Sagamore Spring, located off Williston Road. Native Americans must have depended on this spring in earlier years.

One of the few homes surviving from this early period is the Crowell farmhouse (c. 1690), owned by Paul Crowell in the late 1800s. According to the *Bourne Courier*, this structure was included in the original purchase by the Christian Endeavor Society. After Dr. Francis E. Clark enjoyed his first home on the Bluff, he moved to this old farm. His son Sidney Clark then lived in the original Clark home. Harold and Harriet Clark later owned the Crowell homestead, complete with windmill, until *c*. 1970.

Two

ESTABLISHING A COLONY (1905–1920)

When Rev. Edmund E. Phillips served the Methodist church in Sagamore, he had a vision of a Methodist campground by the pristine shore at Sagamore Beach. Although Phillips had purchased a good-sized bit of land, he had no success in creating any interest among Methodists, perhaps because that denomination already had a flourishing summer colony in the town of Yarmouth. Phillips encountered financial problems and became desperate to sell the land.

It was fortunate for him that a longtime friend, H.L. Chipman, former editor of the *Sagamore Herald*, came to his rescue. Although the paper had ceased publication several decades before, Chipman was still on top of all the news. Called "Omnipresent Chipman" by Sydney Clark, Chipman was aware that at Monument Beach six people from the Christian Endeavor movement, headed by George Coleman, were looking for a site to establish a summer colony. After a good sales pitch, Chipman persuaded Coleman to visit the Phillips property. One summer day, Coleman and his nephew Carville Hands bicycled to the Sandwich railway station and then the two miles beyond, across the causeway to the Bluff. Impressed by the beauty of the beach with its background of dunes and wooded land, Coleman made an enthusiastic report to his friends at Monument Beach. The result was a visit by a committee from Christian Endeavor headquarters in Boston. The members were all as excited as Coleman.

On April 19, 1904, a large group of Christian Endeavor members came by special train from Boston to Sagamore, where according to the *Yarmouth Register* of June 4, 1905, "scores of vehicles of every description" were waiting. "The long string of carriages started for the seashore, headed by J.J. Ryder, a Grand Army veteran, on his famous Kentucky thoroughbred." After a luncheon of fish chowder, provided by Phillips and served in a fisherman's hut, the clergyman answered many questions. He must have been a good salesman, for according to Clark, as the group left to board the train, Phillips was told that members had agreed to buy "two hundred acres for twenty thousand dollars. On the return train journey the money was pledged, with no one putting more than two thousand dollars into the kitty. It was agreed to form Sagamore Beach Company and Hiram Lathrop was appointed Managing Director."

The firm of Whitman and Howard was given the job of surveying, landscaping, and laying out the roads. By the spring of 1905, prospective residents scrambled to obtain choice lots on the Bluff on which to build their cottages. Lumber merchant George W. Stone was the first to complete his cottage, now owned by the Doran family. Coleman raced neck in neck with Lathrop to finish next, with Lathrop winning by one week. Thirteen others soon followed, including Prof. Amos R. Wells, longtime managing editor of the *Christian Endeavor World*. Another cottage builder was Rev. Dr. Francis E. Clark, founder and president of the Christian Endeavor movement.

Meanwhile, plans were under way nearby for a very different entity. After almost two centuries of speculation, beginning with the Pilgrims, Miles Standish, and Gov. William Bradford, the creation of the Cape Cod Canal was imminent.

Looking toward the Highlands, this view of Sagamore Beach could easily be the same as what the new colonists saw before the construction of the Sagamore Beach Colony began. (Courtesy of Town of Sandwich Archives.)

Rev. Dr. Frances E. Clark was the founder of the Christian Endeavor movement. He is shown here with his wife, Harriet (Abbott) Clark. Clark was also president of the Sagamore Beach Colony Club in 1915.

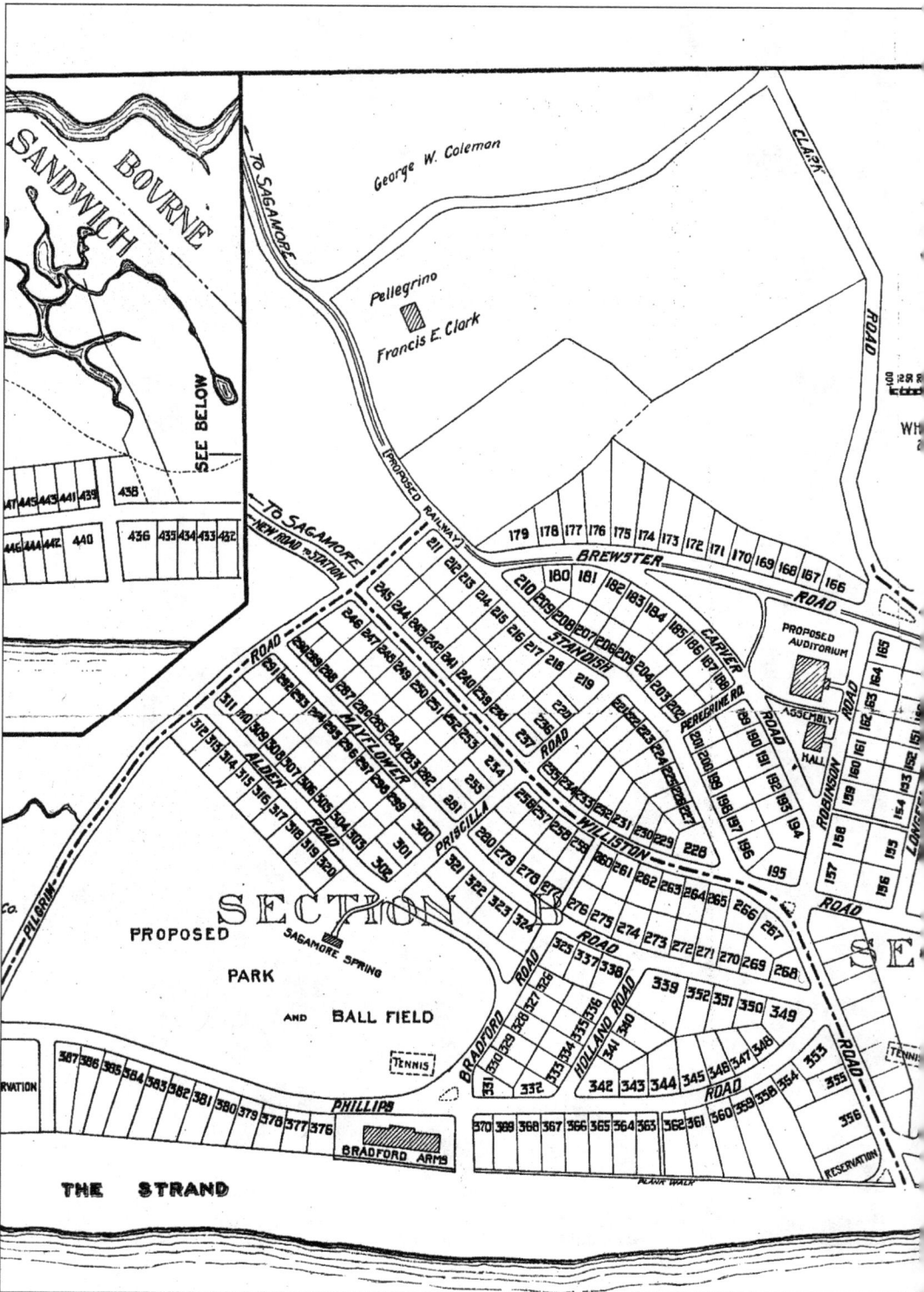

This extensive plot plan of the lands of the Sagamore Beach Company, issued in 1911, shows

N OF LANDS

=OF=

ORE BEACH CO.

ORE BEACH, MASS.

— 1911 —

INDEX MAP

Engineers.
oston.

NAUSETT ROAD

WAMSUTTA

TECUMSEH

ROAD

Fairmount Park

RESERVATION

MANOMET ROAD

[PROPOSED RAILWAY]

WATER TOWER

RESERVATION

WAMPANOAG ROAD

SECTION D

WILLITON ROAD

POST OFFICE & SAGAMORE SHOP

COHASSET RD.

SAGAMORE

SAGAMORE LODGE

TECUMSEH

SHAWMUT

CATAPULT ROAD

ALGONQUIN

MASSASOIT

SAMOSET

Williams

SAGAMORE ROAD

BATH HOUSE

PLANK WALK

THE STRAND

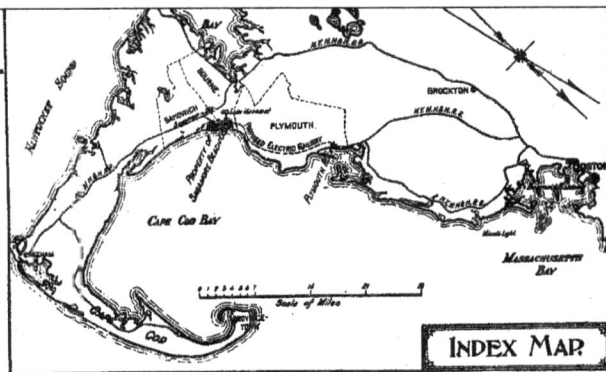

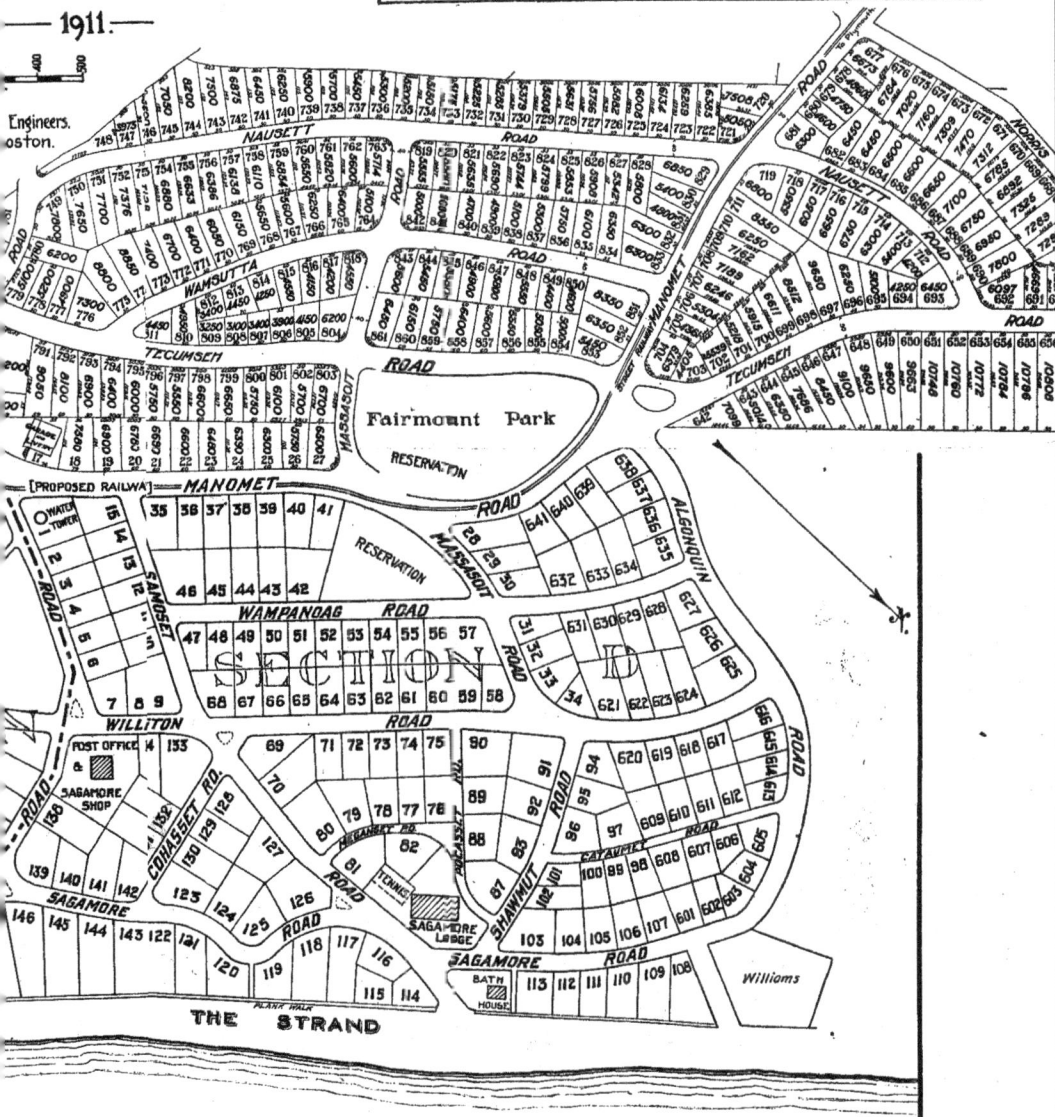

confidence in future sales.

The dory on the beach is the only sign of life on the strand, although it was no doubt the focus of activity later. (Courtesy of Town of Sandwich Archives.)

SAGAMORE BEACH. FROM BEN LOMOND GOLF CLUB.
SAGAMORE, MASS. FEB. 22, 1915.

Golf has been a very important part of activities through the years, beginning with the development of the colony. The Ben Lomond course formally opened in May 1915, on Williston Road near Scusset Beach. (Courtesy of Town of Sandwich Archives.)

There is more activity on the beach in this image and a view of the Sagamore Lodge in the distance. (Courtesy of Town of Sandwich Archives.)

Sagamore Hill (left) was the headquarters of the U.S. Army during World War II. Its gun batteries protected the eastern entrance of the canal, while the U.S. Coast Guard handled the canal's operation and security, according to *The Military History of the Cape Cod Canal*, by Gerald Butler. (Courtesy of Town of Sandwich Archives.)

This small building on the corner of Clark and Williston Roads served as both the Sagamore Beach Company office and the first post office. The Dunlap cottage can be seen in the rear.

In a later photograph (c. 1910), the first building has now expanded with an office and a store.

Seen in a 1908 postcard, Assembly Hall, on Robinson Road, was built in 1907 for meetings and conferences. It was later named Clark Hall after Harold Clark, the longtime treasurer of the Sagamore Beach Colony Club. In recent years, it has served as headquarters for the summer day camp. (Courtesy of Barbara D. Sullivan.)

Sagamore Highland ladies enjoy the beach. (Courtesy of Bourne Historical Center and Archives.)

Sagamore Lodge, Sagamore Beach, Mass.

In 1906, the impressive Sagamore Lodge was built as a center for community activities. This 1910 postcard was printed in Germany and required a 1¢ stamp. The lodge served the community until it was destroyed in a spectacular fire in April 1974.

Another view depicts the Sagamore Lodge in its glory days. The Donovan-Redmond cottage is visible to the right.

24

The cottages on the Bluff are seen from the vantage point of the Sagamore Lodge, to the right.

Frank Sorenti poses in 1938 in front of the Sorenti Brothers gasoline station, at the Sagamore rotary where the state garage is today.

The original houses on the Bluff include, from left to right, the Coleman, Adams, Lane, Morgan, George Doran, Stanton, and John Doran houses. The Coleman cottage was torn down in 2002, but all the others remain.

Although the Coleman house no longer stands, here is a picture of its interior, which gives an example of the decor of these cottages.

Oceanfront cottages of that early era (c. 1917) show the Victorian influence.

The post office and store are shown with two of the popular early automobiles parked in front.

The Bradford Arms, a "good-sized and delightful shore hotel" according to Sidney Clark, was built in 1908. It hosted many guests until it was destroyed by fire in 1935.

This interior photograph of the Bradford Arms shows the various amenities available to guests.

The view depicted on this postcard, postmarked July 3, 1907, is of the Bradford Arms. The postcard bears a 1¢ stamp featuring Benjamin Franklin.

The first Polar Bear Club is shown in 1916, with the dunking plank in the foreground.

When the Colony Club was organized on a permanent basis in September 1909, one of the first projects was laying out the Playstead. Along with tennis and other games, the Punch Society sociable took place every Saturday afternoon. "Punch was ladled out from a stone jar into several dozen mugs, but you may be sure it was never 'spiked' . . . In those tee-totaling days we distilled our own fun and brewed games solely by our wits," noted founder Rev. Dr. Frances E. Clark.

In the early days of ladies' tennis at the Playstead, the games were played in billowing skirts.

Notice the absence of trees and the large tent in this early Playstead photograph.

The younger residents were not forgotten at the Playstead. The gazebo, with its impressive view of Cape Cod Bay, was a dandy place to relax.

This *c.* 1910 photograph of Sydney Clark making music as a young boy was sent with his Christmas card in 1973.

Bathing was a community enterprise at 11:00 a.m. each day.

Participants in the first Colony Day in 1911 were awakened by the town crier as he went the rounds calling, "Hear Ye! Hear Ye! All good people of Sagamore Beach," and announcing the program for the day.

Residents are gathered for the July 4, 1910 celebration in front of the post office and store.

Some Pilgrims relax during Colony Days. Note the bass drum to the right.

Ladies and gentlemen are shown at a gathering at Hawes Field c. 1910.

This picture of carefree youth on a Labor Day weekend was contributed by Clark Fisher, shown here at the far lower right. Two of the group are unidentified, but the others include Barbara Banks, Gordon Sleeper, Betty Stevenson, Doug Everett, and Barbara Grissidick. (Courtesy of Clark Fisher.)

36

Frank and Mabel Batchelder are shown here with their children. The children are, from left to right, Theron, Catherine (seated on floor), Watts, and Joe Batchelder.

The Gillis family is shown c. 1930 on the front porch of the Batchelder house, on Standish Road. From left to right are Barbara Gillis, Tom Gillis, Gloria (Zickell) Gillis, and Gertrude Gillis. Tom Gillis was the driver for Mabel Batchelder, a well-known National Republican Committee member.

Mira Adams married Frank Howell on June 12, 1920, at Assembly Hall. There is no record of any other wedding celebrated in Assembly Hall. Shown here are, from left to right, Rev. Francis E. Clark, unidentified, Harold Clark, Frank Howell, Mira Adams, Harriet Clark, and unidentified. (Courtesy of Anne Allen.)

Sagamore Beach Marriages

Alice Whitcomb and Gram Pope
Elizabeth Sage and Joe Bachelder
Jeannine Garrity and Dick Holway
John Doran and Susan Fisher
Barbara Johnson and Dick Newell
Ann Howell and Charlie Allen
Tim Traub and Harriet Congdon
Joe Sullivan and Lynn Pritchard
Michael McKenna and Linda Zarella
Suzanne Mattaliano and John Garrity
Gregory Fayne and Majorie Pritchard
Malcolm Banks and Jane MacNeill
Norman Hill and Bernice Kendall
Joan Erkkila and Frank Fayne
Lynn Keery and Keith Ellis
Wellesley Hannington and Barbara Schlicht
Francis K. Howell and Janet Banks
Jeff Redman and Jane Ahern

Three

THE CAPE COD CANAL

Sagamore Beach residents had an excellent opportunity to see the construction of the Cape Cod Canal. Sydney Clark wrote, "As early as 1909 Henry Upham used to take us in his sailboat to watch the first big stones from Blue Hill, Maine being dumped into the water to form the breakwater."

The idea of severing the "canal from the continent" had been thought about in the Pilgrim era. It was also recommended by George Washington and mentioned through the intervening years. It was not actually attempted, however, until 1870, when a charter was granted by the Massachusetts General Court to Alpheus Hardy of the Cape Cod Ship Canal. Studies and planning took so much time that the charter was in danger of being revoked. Apparently, in order to show that action had begun, a rather strange event occurred. On September 15, 1880, about 500 Italians arrived and started digging, using shovels and wheelbarrows. Then, apparently, funding ran out, and the bosses disappeared. In mid-October, the men marched into the town center, causing a panic when there was only one interpreter to explain the problem. Calm descended when the selectman arranged for the distribution of food, and the governor of Massachusetts arranged to transport the men to New York City.

In June 1883, some of Hardy's previous partners received a new charter. They contracted with Frederick Lockwood to begin dredging at the canal's east end. This Lockwood dredge was the one the Boston legislators had seen at work. Although the company had an extension in 1887, funding again ran out. To the rescue came wealthy New Yorker August Belmont, who was interested in the project because his Perry ancestors came from Cape Cod and he realized lives and shipping would be saved if it was carried out. According to *The Military History of Cape Cod*, by Gerald Butler, Belmont took over the Boston Cape Cod and New York Canal Company, which had been granted a charter in 1899. Work began on the canal on June 19, 1909.

The new residents of Sagamore Beach had front-row seats, because the work began on the canal's east end. They could watch the channel's progression as it cut between the Swift Memorial Methodist Church and the Keith Car and Manufacturing Company. They could also appreciate the new small drawbridge over the old causeway. There is no doubt that many residents enjoyed the festivities when the waterway opened in 1914, with the accompaniment of an elaborate pageant. When the federal government purchased the Cape Cod Canal in 1928, a larger drawbridge was erected, as were the Sagamore, Bourne, and railroad bridges in 1933–1935.

Sydney Clark wrote, "Naturally we at the beach watched all these developments with considerable excitement. . . . Though the Cape and the Continent were indeed severed by the construction of the Canal, yet paradoxically the new and newer bridges united them more securely than ever before."

This was a period of change on land as well. At first, Sagamore Beach was called Scusset and was in the town of Sandwich. Later, the area was called West Sandwich but was still part of Sandwich. When the town divided in 1884, it became Sagamore, then Sagamore Beach, and belonged to Bourne.

The three bridges of the Cape Cod Canal are shown in this aerial view. The cut of the canal was eight miles. The approaches were five miles, and the original depth was 25 feet below mean low water. The original width was 100 feet. Later, it had a 32-foot mean low water depth and was 540 feet wide. This image was included in the *Fiftieth Anniversary Program of Cape Cod Canal Bridges 1935–1985*. (Photograph by U.S. Corps of Engineers, courtesy of Cape Cod Community College Archives.)

Cutting the Last Dike in
Cape Cod Canal, Apr., 1914

August Belmont and a distinguished party watch the cutting of the last dike when the Cape
Cod Canal was opened in April 1914.

In this view, August Belmont and William Parsons shake hands after the waters from the two
bays flowed together.

Pictured here is the Bridge Street drawbridge, at the Sagamore crossing of the Cape Cod Canal.

The road from the village is seen from the old Canal Bridge. Note the Hoxie School and Savery Avenue in the background.

A four-pipe destroyer cruises through the Cape Cod Canal, with the Keith plant in the background. The Keith plant extended along the canal for over a mile.

A destroyer passes through the canal under the Sagamore drawbridge near the Keith plant. The Keith family, particularly Malvina Keith, was very involved in Sagamore Beach affairs.

In 1933, the cement footings for the present Sagamore Bridge were erected. The car belongs to Frank Sorenti, and at the right is Luigi Sorenti.

The completed Sagamore Bridge is shown at its opening in 1935.

This aerial view of the new Sagamore Bridge, taken above Sagamore Beach, also shows the old Sagamore Bridge at the far left, as well as the old Keith plant. The image was included in the official program *Opening Cape Cod Canal Bridges*. (Photograph by U.S. Corps of Engineers, courtesy of Cape Cod Community College Archives.)

A tall ship passes under the railroad bridge in 1992.

The Keith Car and Manufacturing Company is seen here from Savery Avenue, across the Cape Cod Canal. Begun in 1846 as Keith and Ryder to manufacture carriages, stagecoaches, and prairie schooners, the company developed at the turn of the century into a plant over a mile long, employing several hundred men to build freight cars.

Swift Memorial Church (dedicated in 1911), the third church building, was built when heavy equipment was not available. Church secretary Pat Weaver wrote in a brief history of the church, "Every stone had to be carried to the site by horse-drawn carts, in wheelbarrows, in baskets, and even carried in the arms of parishioners."

Four

LIFE IN THE COLONY (1920–1955)

The fledgling Sagamore Beach Company had grown by leaps and bounds, which must have surprised the settlers already there. According to Sydney Clark in *Sagamore Beach Colony, the First Fifty Years,* "before the first summer, there were only seven small houses here, used for the most part by fishermen. Several of them, improved almost beyond recognition, were still in use by cottagers."

The first 15 years had seen the major buildings erected. The Sagamore Lodge was built in 1906 and served as a community center until Assembly Hall was built in 1907. The large seaside resort hotel Bradford Arms was built in 1908, and a bathhouse that was used by everyone was completed in front of the Sagamore Lodge. A boardwalk was built on the strand between the two hotels, noted Clark. (The boardwalk was destroyed by storms twice and replaced twice, but the storms were so strong that the nor'easters prevailed.)

About this time, the Playstead was laid out with two tennis courts and grounds for quoits, badminton, tetherball, and later roque (similar to croquet). A post office and the Little Store were established, and later a laundry was added. Once a strong, never-failing spring of pure water was located, it replaced several wells, and the water company standpipe was always filled. These were most of the places open to the public in the early years.

From the beginning, Sagamore Beach was definitely a religious community, "with ministers galore and religious editors and authors at every turn," according to Sidney Clark. At first a mammoth tent sheltered Christian Endeavor institutes, Sunday school conferences, and meetings of Friends (Quakers). By 1907, the large gatherings met in the new Assembly Hall. Resident George Coleman, who was then president of the Ford Hall Forum in Boston, arranged for an annual sociological conference to be held at Sagamore Beach during the years from 1908 to 1917. The meetings in Assembly Hall must have been lively: An address given in 1910 was titled "The Saloon from the Liquor Dealer's Point of View."

Every morning rain or shine, the whole community gathered at 11:00 a.m. at the beach for a swim. Sailing, tennis tournaments, baseball, and popular music concerts varied the days. A young people's group known as "the Bunch" used to hike to Scusset Creek, Peaked Cliff, Cedarville, and Lake Manomet, where the Sagamore Beach Company owned a camp for colony use. In those adventurous days before automobiles, wrote Clark, "if we felt an urge for a chocolate or strawberry soda, we would think nothing of walking to the nearest drug store in Sandwich, or to the old fish house north of Scusset Creek's outlet where Tinker mackerel cost two cents each and lobsters were just as cheap."

Since 1909, the Sagamore Beach Colony Club has watched over the colony, establishing the annual Colony Days, a special time each year when the whole community celebrated. A typical day began with the ringing of the town crier's bell, followed by water and land sports in the morning; children's games at the post office at noon; then dinner and open house, with everybody parading in costume (mostly Pilgrim or Native American) to the Dell for the play. Then the kettledrum was played at the post office, and the old folks concert was presented at night. The Colony Days were held annually until 1922. After that they were held intermittently, usually featuring children and youths.

The club was also active in zoning. As a result, the business areas were located near the Sagamore Bridge, leaving the rest of the area quietly residential. By the time of the 50-year celebration, there were 140 cottages on the beach. Forty of these families were living year-round. Interestingly, that is the exact number of cottages built in the first year.

Many changes occurred during those years, a harbinger of things to come. The most dramatic was the change in the landscape with the building of the canal in 1914. In this period, many inventions appeared (although not all were welcomed). Telephones and radios were enthusiastically received, but automobiles and electricity were sometimes looked at askance. The former were feared by owners of horses and buggies, while the latter made people wonder whether it was safe. One woman in a nearby area made sure her son used the light switches first, and then welcomed the new lights excitedly when she saw that he was safe. In the 1930s came the new Sagamore Bridge, Bourne Bridge, and Railroad Bridge. Less welcome were the two world wars, in which many young people of Sagamore Beach did their part.

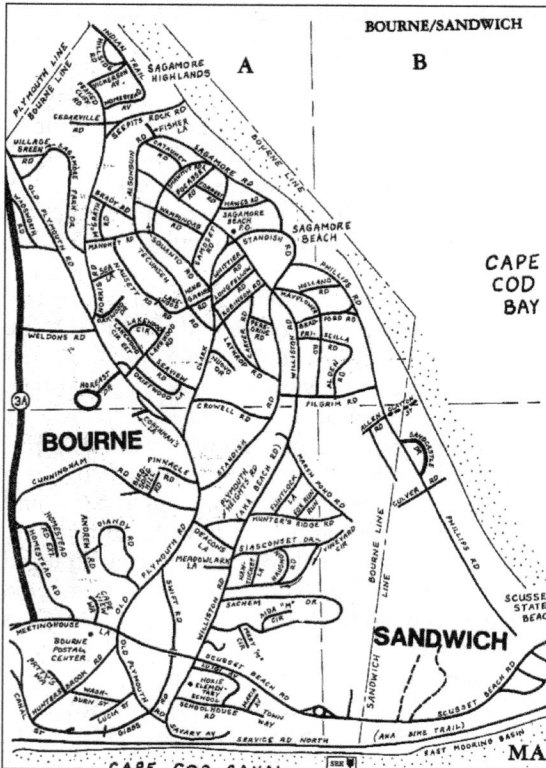

Featured in *Cape Cod's Finest Atlas*, this map of Bourne's Sagamore Beach village shows the boundaries as everything above the north bank of the Cape Cod Canal, except for a wedge at the right, which is in Sandwich. To the far right is Cape Cod Bay. At the top is the Plymouth line, and to the right is Route 3A. (Courtesy of Meg Maps.)

The bathhouse was just in front of the Sagamore Lodge. It was swept out to sea in the 1938 hurricane.

The number of people had also grown. Here there is a three-legged race in progress at a Fourth of July celebration in front of the post office.

The Sagamore Lodge is pictured before the bathhouse "went to sea."

This view shows the Bradford Arms to the left, with the Keery house to the right. (Courtesy of Town of Sandwich Archives.)

Here is a view of Sagamore Road, which is familiar today, although the road is now paved. (Courtesy of Town of Sandwich Archives.)

A more extensive view of summer residences gives evidence of the continuing growth. (Courtesy of Town of Sandwich Archives.)

"Sorenti" has been a familiar name at the Sagamore circle for years. Here, Frank Sorenti is seen with Joe Sorenti Jr. in 1935.

For a time, the Sorenti family owned the Sagamore Lodge. Pictured here in the 1930s are the ladies of the cleaning crew. From left to right, they are Lena Hamington, Lena Sorenti (wife of Pat), Rose Sorenti, and Regina Tontini.

Someone has come for the weekend at the Sagamore Lodge and left the car out front.

Guests dressed for dinner at the Bradford Arms include Mrs. Harrington, Katherine Burn, and Eleanor Vorhees. These ladies would arrive on the New York boat and stay at the hotel for extended periods each summer.

Youngsters were always an important part of the community. Pictured are Richard and Russell Locke, grandsons of Oscar Thayer, who designed the Sagamore Lodge.

Charles and Rachel Allen are about to depart for the tennis courts in 1931.

These youngsters, pictured c. 1933 at the Pillars (then owned by the Green family), include Gracie Green, Rachel Allen, Charles Allen, and John Reynolds Hammett.

Benjamin Percy Arnold plays cards at his home on Williston Road in 1924.

A raft and sailboats are visible in the distance in this 1933 view. (Courtesy of Norman Hill.)

Youngsters are shown on the raft in 1933. This was the meeting place for most teenagers. (Courtesy of Norman Hill.)

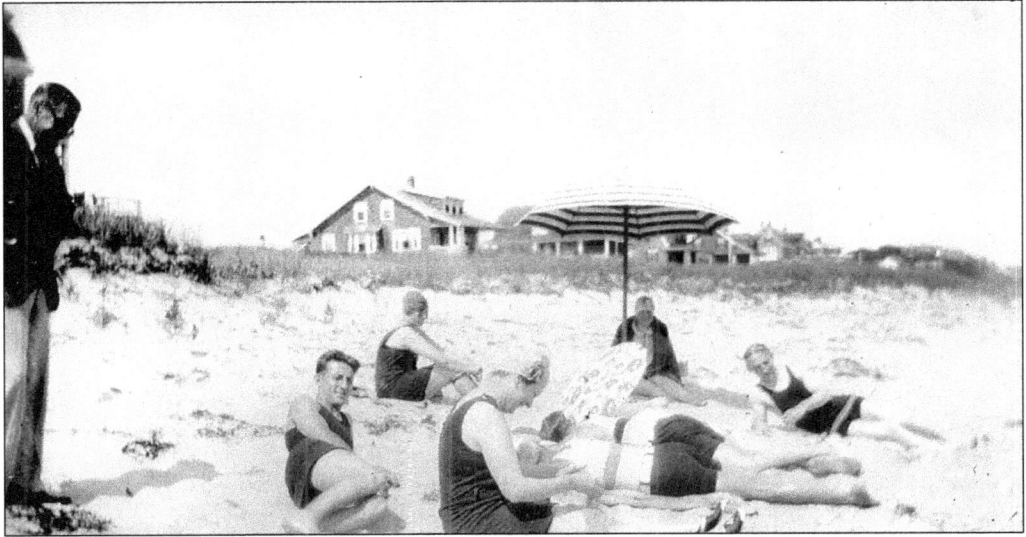

Guests at the Bradford Arms are summoned to dinner.

Champe Fisher and Malcolm Banks are shown about to go to sea in 1933.

The beach offers a variety of views in different seasons. Here the parking lot at Doyle's beach is shown in the spring of 1933.

In the 1930s, ever-present erosion and the remains of the boardwalk could be seen.

Malcolm Banks is seen here on the post office steps in 1943.

This picture looking north shows the ice formations at Sagamore Beach during a winter in the 1930s.

The Soule boat, a gaff-rigged sailboat, was destroyed by a sudden overnight storm on Labor Day weekend in 1933.

The fish weirs could be seen off the beach from the 1930s to the 1950s. (Courtesy of Norman Hill.)

Here the fisherman are filling their nets at the weirs in the 1930s. (Courtesy of Norman Hill.)

Members of the Lacey clan take a ride on Hawes Road in their vintage machine in the 1930s. They are, from left to right, Rachel Lacey, Margie Lacey, Lila Bob Lacey, Ben Lacey, and unidentified.

Brian McNealey (lower right), who had a career later as a prizefighter, is shown c. 1950 on the jetty with friends.

A ball game at Hawes Field in 1933 shows Clark Fisher at bat. (Courtesy of Norman Hill.)

Peg Donahue (left) admires two-year-old Peggy Ann Donahue, along with onlookers, at the beach in 1941.

In this 1943 Colony Club dance scene are pictured, from left to right, Barbara Johnson, Dudley Durgin, Rachel Allen, Lee Bergstrom, Franny Bird, and Wellesley Hannington.

Guys (not dolls) *c.* 1943 in the Dell are, from left to right, Don Gleason, Dick Andrews, Paul Nichols, Dick Holway, Don MacNeil, and Champe Fisher.

Youths on the beach *c.* 1955 include Janice Van Wart, Margie Doyle, Mary Doyle, Mary Doran, David Garrity, Joe Sergi, Barbara Futnam, Ham Chapin, Frank Trainor, Peggy Donahue, Carol Trainor, Freddie Adams, JoAnne Van Wart, Kathy Doran, Barbara Doran, Beth Tranor, Dukie Doyle, Georgie Doran, Tom Kane, and Steve Garrity.

The guys on the beach here *c.* 1954 are, from left to right, Steve Garrity, Carl Compagne, John Kane, Freddy Adams, David Garrity, Frank Trainor, Bobby Trainor, Richard Kane, Tommy Kane, and Joe Sergi.

One of the Newell girls exercises her horse at the family complex at the foot of Bradford Road, with the Newell house visible in the background.

The grounds at Wyndacre were owned and operated by the Newell family in 1934.

The stable at Wyndacre is pictured in 1934.

There were also workhorses at Sagamore Beach, as evidenced by the men with the ice wagons who could be seen in the 1920s and 1930s.

At summer Colony Days from 1908 to 1938, residents performed plays in the Dell, ranging from Shakespearean dramas to a mock town meeting.

Thespians in the Dell are pictured in a less friendly moment.

A resident portrays a Pilgrim
who arrived in 1620.

Colony Day entertainers are seen
in a lighter moment.

Lila Allen and Rachel Allen are getting ready for Colony Day in 1930.

Genevieve Clark Fisher is shown here at age 14. She died in 1981 at age 91, having been an American Red Cross worker in World War I, a teacher, and a suffragette.

This photograph of Sagamore Beach beauties was published in the *Boston Globe* in 1946, after a letter was received from Donald Fisher, Dick Holway, and Don MacNeil, complaining that there were no girls at the beach. From left to right are the following: (front row) Patti (Carroll) Conway, Sue (Bergstom) Campbell, and Joanne (Carroll) Maker; (back row) Betty Tatra, Jeanne (Stanley) Wurlitper, Jeannine (Garrity) Holway, Barbara (Schlicht) Hannington, Carson (Barnes) Fleming, and Rachel (Allen) Fagerburg. (Courtesy of the *Boston Globe*.)

This aerial view of the fishing pier at Scusset is a reminder of the part this place played in the lives of Sagamore Beach people through the years—even though it was still in the town of Sandwich. (Courtesy of Bourne Historical Center and Archives.)

An aerial view of the Sagamore Beach side of the Sagamore Bridge illustrates how the business areas clustered around one of the gateways to Cape Cod. (Courtesy of Bourne Historical Center and Archives.)

Five

LIFE IN THE COLONY (1955–PRESENT)

The 50th-anniversary celebration of Sagamore Beach Colony, held on Colony Day on August 13, 1955, was a festive affair. The usual Colony Day schedule was followed, culminating with a gala evening banquet featuring resident Hon. Joseph W. Martin Jr., who complimented the club on keeping alive family traditions. Mrs. Eben S.S. Keith reminisced about early Sagamore, the construction of the Cape Cod Canal, and the tie between the village and the beach. A memorable skit, *Golden Glances*, followed, and then a musical was presented, with Harold Clark playing the ukulele and Sydney Clark on the violin.

In 1980, a 75th-anniversary booklet by Dottie and Don Clark, Muriel and Henry Pappas, and Frannie Tidemarsh filled in the intervening years. It noted that the entertainment committee had arranged for canal cruises, bridge tournaments, golf classics, tennis tournaments, and sailing races (although the O'Day Sprites had given way to Sunfish). There was now a junior tennis tournament as well as the senior tournament.

Physical changes have occurred, with the addition of approximately 100 new homes. One of the most dramatic changes occurred in the spring of 1974, when the Sagamore Lodge went up in flames. The wind fortunately blew off the land, so no other buildings were lost.

According to Beverly Niit in *Sagamore Beach at the Century Mark*, in 1976 Heimar Niit was president during the national bicentennial. She wrote, "An immigrant himself, he recognized the need to document our own history and introduced the first yearbook which contained summer calendar events with names and addresses of members."

When a tennis professional was hired in 1980, matches were exchanged with nearby clubs. Monday night bridge, a reintroduced reading circle, and a summer day camp of about 100 neighborhood youngsters kept people busy. Fundraising events have included a dinner auction hosted by Jack Williams of the local Channel 4 television station, Little Joe Cook dance parties, and around-the-world culinary presentations. Dramas continued to be performed, such as the 1983 reenactment of Sagamore Beach history with George Burke playing a judge who almost refuses the application for citizenship made by the character played by Heimar Niit, as well as a dinner theater presentation, *The Case of the Sagamore Shipwreck*, in 1992.

Beverly Niit also notes that children and traditions continue to thrive, particularly at the day camp. A teen tennis program was begun for the older group (those who were not quite of working-permit age). Those of camping age, with professional directors in place, would begin their day at 9:00 a.m., bring their lunch, and head for home at 1:00 p.m. Swimming, tennis, field games, arts and crafts, and teamwork were, and continue to be, the essence of the eight-week program.

A first-grader could conceivably progress through the delights of making sand castles, experiencing an archeological dig, participating in a scavenger hunt, or taking field trips to other Cape Cod attractions. Many could then join the junior tennis team, while becoming junior counselors. By the college years, the same person could move on to become assistant director and, after college, camp director.

"Many more campers have moved on to successful careers, engendered by the camp lessons of cooperation and teamwork," Beverly Niit noted, "not to mention the stage presence gained by participation in the final extravaganza—the Camp Show."

The 50th anniversary of the colony in 1955 was a gala affair at Assembly Hall. At the head table are, from left to right, George J. Doran Sr., an unidentified woman, Harold Clark, Harriet Clark, Frederick G. Fisher Sr., Malvina Keith (behind the flowers), Sydney Clark (standing), Joseph P. Martin, Genevive Fisher, three unidentified women, and president John Neall.

Sydney Clark (left) and Harold Clark play for the 50th-anniversary guests in 1955, as Frederick G. Fisher Sr. and Malvina Keith look over the crowd.

This photograph of an annual Sagamore Beach Colony picnic shows remains of the boardwalk that once connected the Sagamore Lodge and the Bradford Arms.

The boys shown c. 1958 are, from left to right, Bob Tennant, unidentified, Don Holway, Rick Holway, Wally Tennant, Steven Fisher, Dick Holway, Hamilton Fisher, and Tom Mahoney.

Andy Anderson (right) went from ice-cream man to Sagamore Beach Colony Club president. Shown with Anderson in 1962 at Cataumet are, from left to right, an unidentified person and Ruth, Martin, Frank, and John Anderson.

Shown, from left to right, are Rachel Allen, Skipper Baker, and Ruth Howard Baker relaxing on the beach (in foreground), while Andrea Baker (with braid) is visible in the background.

Residents and friends are enjoying the 1958 clambake on the beach.

The Anderson boys are pictured here in 1959. They are, from left to right, Frank Anderson, John Anderson, and Martin Anderson.

Ruth Messer Anderson of Norwich, Connecticut, mother of Frank, John, and Martin Anderson, sits in front of her Sagamore Beach garden in 1968.

Guys and dolls c. 1955 are pictured on the beach. The dolls are, from left to right, Mary Doran, Marge Doyle, Mary Doyle, Joanne Van Wart, Peggy Donahue, Janice Van Wart, Carol Trainor, Barbara Putnam, and Nancy Kane. The guys are, from left to right, John Kane, Joe Sergi, Carl Campagne, Freddy Adams, Hove Chapin, David Garrity, and unidentified.

Freddie Adams, John Kane, and Frank Trainor are about to break into song in 1954.

Eleanor's Restaurant, pictured here in the 1950s after it was moved to Meeting House Road, was a favorite neighborhood restaurant featuring home-baked pies.

This is a view of the Sorenti Brothers gas station at the Sagamore rotary.

The Sagamore Lodge was a spectacular sight as it burned in the spring of 1974. (Courtesy of James Craig.)

Neighbors breathed sighs of relief that the prevailing wind that day was blowing straight off the land when the Sagamore Lodge burned. Otherwise, more buildings could have burned. (Courtesy of James Craig.)

The Sagamore Beach campers are pictured in 1963. They are, left to right, as follows: (first row) Mary Jane Tuohy, Ann Fagerburg, Rudy Fagerburg, Karen Fagerburg, Cammie Eckart, Margo Burke, Allison Hill, Jessica Fitch, John Anderson, Sue LaCroix, Candy Fisher, Seth Pappas, Frank Anderson, and Bobby Leferts; (second row) Andrea Baker, Linda Paliuca, Sally Baer, David Hill, Peter Fayne, Martin Anderson, Steve LaCroix, Vicky Massard, Bruce Eckardt,

Pam Massard, and Jeannine LaCroix; (third row) Bon Donovan, David Forest, Paul Zickell, Mike Ryan, Ginger Read, Ruth Erkkila, Sue Seimon, Valerie Eckardt, Julie Fitch, Christina Pappas, JoAnn Fayne, John Doran, Malcolm Hill, Mark Foley, George Doran, Patty Mora, Dede Mora, and Peter Zickell; (fourth row) Tommy Zickell, John Tuohy, John Hughes (camp director), Barbara Doran (assistant camp director), and Mike MacDonald (tennis coach).

At this costume party, the angel, Rita MacDonald (president of the Colony Club, 1962–1963), begs for mercy from George Burke, who plays Caesar.

Former Sagamore Beach Colony Club president Fred Fisher performs in a Colony Club skit.

The camp show culminates the season with a song-and-dance production at Assembly Hall.

Bob Tennant, who served as Sagamore Beach Colony Club president in 1983–1984, is shown cooling his heels.

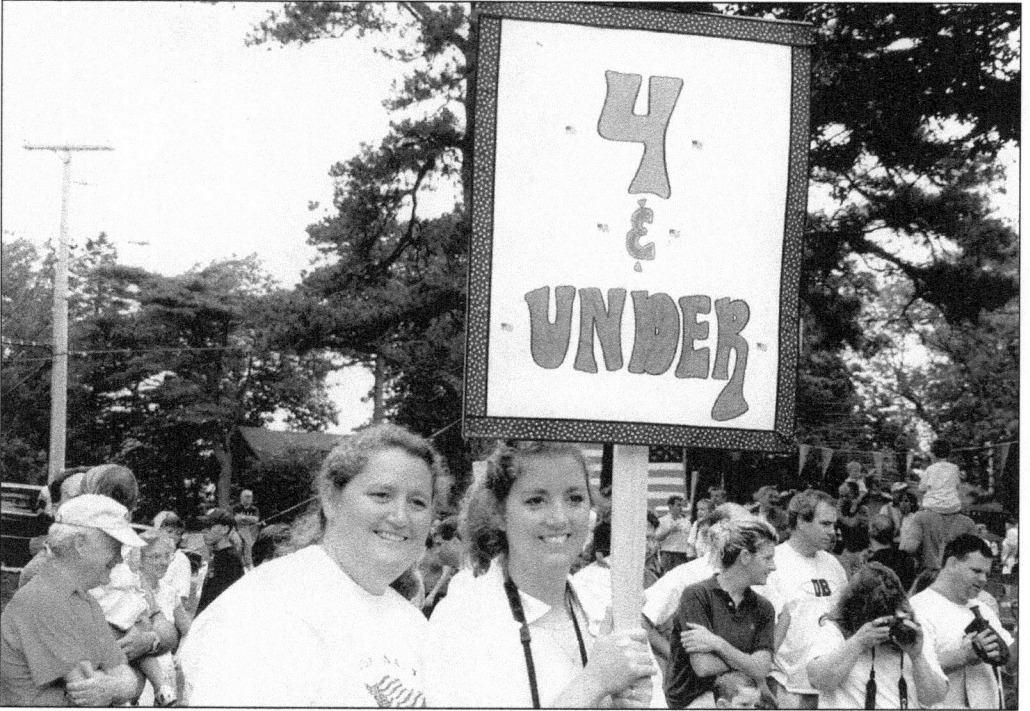

Diane Heller and Suzanne Nicklaus help organize the games for young people at Hawes Field on the Fourth of July.

Contestants are posed for the three-legged race.

Another favorite of the young is the wheelbarrow race.

Campers love to portray in costume "the Spirit of Sagamore Beach."

These beach boys are, from left to right, Donald Gleason, Robert Gleason, Russell Locke, and Richard Locke.

Seth Pappas and Rick Fisher are ready for spear fishing.

Hamilton Fisher and a
friend have found an
anchor on the beach.
It is now residing in
Talia Fisher's yard.

Frank and John Anderson wonder if this boat will float.

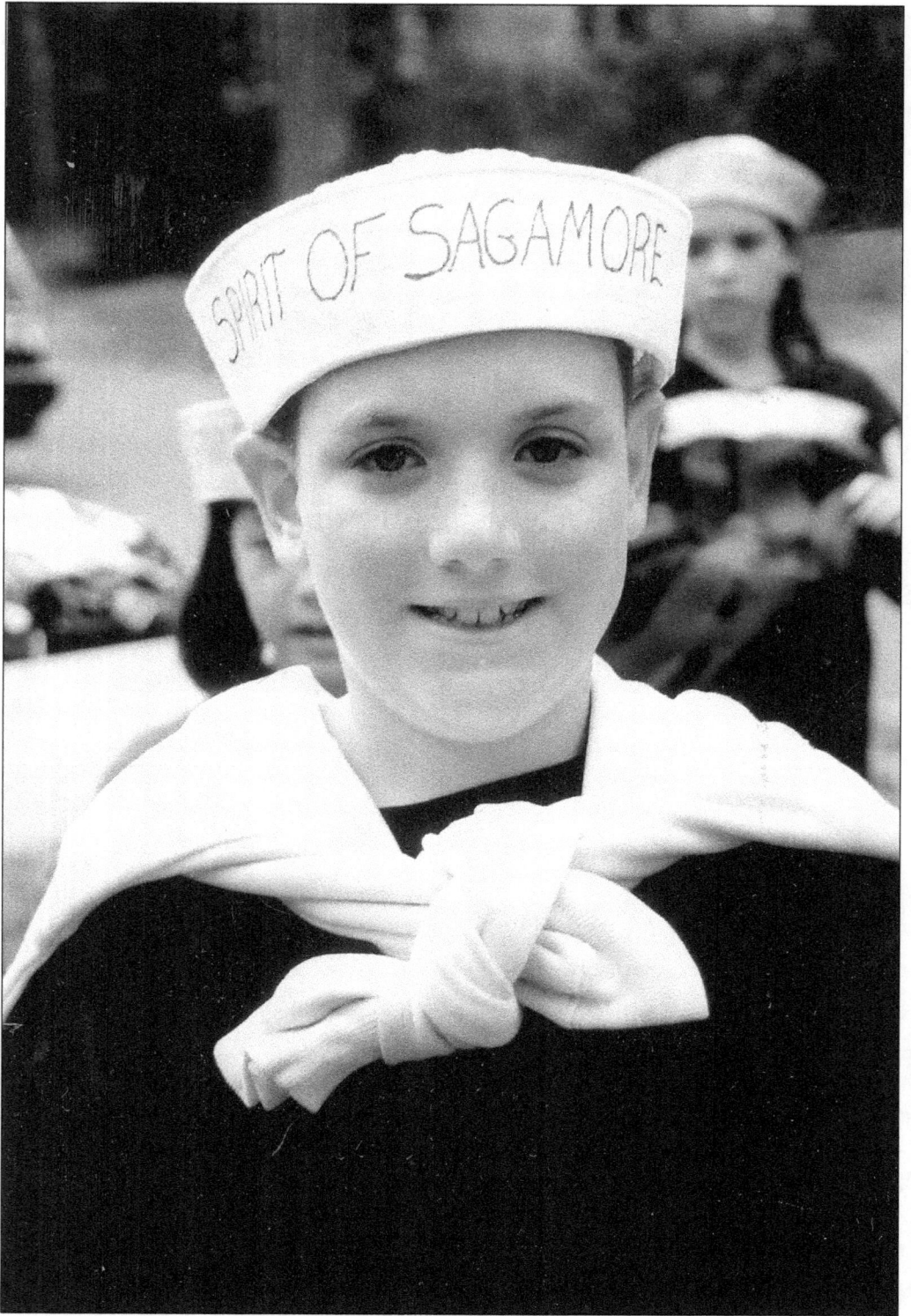

Pat McCahill, at age nine, is showing the spirit of Sagamore.

Meredith Chase in her lobster hat is great at selling raffle tickets for a giant lobster.

At the Round Hill Golf Tournament in 1973, the participants are, from left to right, as follows: (front row) Rita MacDonald, Bob Reynolds, Eleanor Doran, Paula Mealy, Audrey Wethern, and Peg Parry; (middle row) Bob Parry, Jim Queenan, and Todd Reynolds; (back row) Angie Borelli, Helen Queenan, George Doran Sr., John Dalton, Pearl Dalton, Bob Mealy, George Doherty Jr., Dwight Ware, and Alan Werthen.

In attendance at the Minette Baer Golf Tournament are, from left to right, the following: (front row) Ruth Anderson; (middle row) Eleanor Doran, Evelyn Mora, Rita MacDonald, and Todd Reynolds; (back row) Marge LaCroix, Helen Queenan, Patty Fisher, Jo Buckley, Candy Mattaliano, Paula Mealy, and Connie Keery.

Tailgating in 1975 are, from left to right, Kelly Doherty, grandmother Eleanor Doran, Suzanne Doherty, and Christine Hegenbart.

This group of tennis players from c. 1980 includes, from left to right, Connie Keery, Marge LaCroix, Nette Borelli, Rita MacDonald, Kathleen Hagenbart, Barbara Sullivan, Mary Doherty, Patty Fisher, and Beverly Niit.

The member and guest tennis events in 1980 were good excuses for parties. Three sets of tennis were followed by lunch and much laughter. Pictured, from left to right, are the following: (first row) Debbie O'Dugan, Kathleen Hegenbart, Marilyn Carens, and Candy Mattaliano; (second row) Lynn Pritchard, Sandy Burke, Ann Garzone, Netti Borelli, Marge LaCroix, Rita MacDonald,

Patty Clapp, unidentified, Lynn Salmella, and unidentified; (third row) Fran Tidemarsh, unidentified, Mary Doherty, Beverly Niit, unidentified, Gigi Green, unidentified, unidentified, and Vi Cassasanta; (fourth row) Nan Crossland, Patty Fisher, unidentified, Sue LaCroix, Audrey Werthen, and Alice Werthen.

Dick Holway and Jeannine Garrity express "young love in the teens" in 1943.

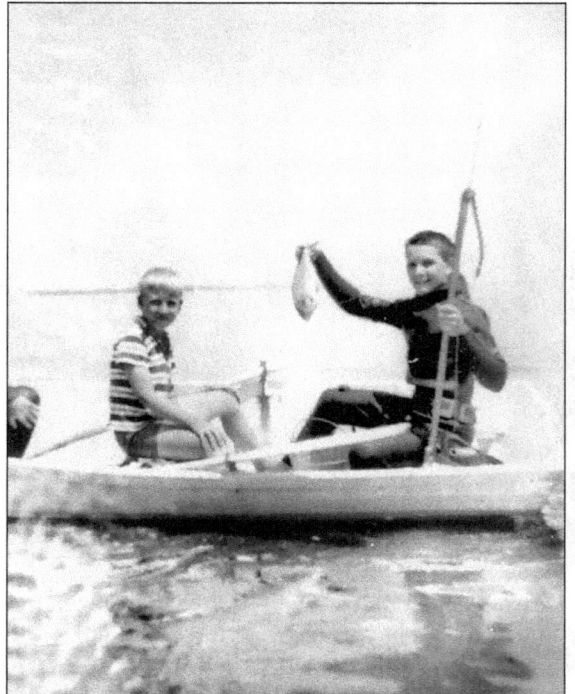

Rick Fisher and Chip Fisher show the big catch after their fishing expedition.

Six

REMINISCENCES, HOMES, AND
FAMILIES OF THE BEACH

"Graham Pope, the postmaster, was the original mentor of sailing at Sagamore Beach around 1930. He rebuilt a classic fishing dory into a complete center-boarded sailboat. He became a hero by sailing across Cape Cod Bay to Provincetown.

"Shortly thereafter the second mentor Harry Sage purchased a little 10-foot plywood beginners' sailboat called a 'Capey.' Several others, including the Fishers, purchased Capeys, and races up and down the beach began. After Harry attended sailing camp he traded up to a sixteen-footer with jib. Again the Fishers followed with a Winnebout, and Douglas Everett and Betsey Riordon purchased their Cape Cod Mercuries. These boats were moored offshore with 150 pound mushroom anchors connected to six-foot bouys. They were a sight to see as they rode out the northeast storms.

"After Word War II interest grew under the third mentor, Dr. Ruth Anderson, who introduced the O'Day Sprite. She organized the Sagamore Beach Yacht Club with weekend races and away challenges with Pocasset and Mashnee Clubs.

"During the 1950s enthusiasm peaked with the fourth mentor, Dr. Norman Hill. Soon there were seven or eight boats participating in weekend races around triangular courses. Under the watchful eyes of those on the committee boat, participants competed for the season's trophy.

"Unfortunately the following generations found other interests and sailing at Sagamore Beach passed into oblivion."

—Clark Fisher, *Sailing, A Once Thriving Sport*

"The beach in front of the Colony was the major area of activity in the 30s. Since most adults were without cars and therefore unable to go to Hyannis or Plymouth, or even go grocery shopping, many of them spent much time on the beach sitting, reading, relaxing, doing handwork, or gathering in small sociable groups. For the teenagers, however, the beach and the raft were the center of our lives. We would get to the beach by 10:00 each morning, go immediately out to the raft for swimming, racing, and diving to explore the bottom for shells, starfish, and sculpins. Or we would swim out to the outer sandbar, which was shallow enough to stand on, and was studded with sand collars. . . . About noon we would go home for lunch and go back to the beach from 2:00 to 5:00 in the afternoon. We all became experienced swimmers.

My grandfather once remarked, 'They're like a school of fish in the water.'"

—Dr. Norman Hill, *The Summers of 1930s at Sagamore*

"Our Colony's survival and growth has been possible because of those who have shouldered the yoke of responsibility and kindled the flames again and again. Some of the almost century old homes still stand on the shores of Sagamore Beach, having weathered the infamous blizzard of 1977 and Hurricane Bob in 1991. So too our nation has weathered the terrorist attack of September 11, 2001. So also has the heart and soul of our colony weathered the years and stood together, drawn closer in human connectedness. Though conflicted with the challenges of modern life and a highly technological world, we continually are inspired and enlightened by our wondrous Jewel on the Bay, returning to our older, more grounded conventions. Surely we understand that family life and mutual support continue to keep the Colony's flame alive. As the tide of our affairs ebbs and flows, we here on our shore continue to hold on dearly to our steadfast love of Sagamore Beach."

—Beverly Niit, *Sagamore Beach at the Century Mark*

"Our Colony has grown up but it hasn't grown old. That's the advantage it has over us frail human beings who can't seem to manage the one without submitting to the other. It is our hope and belief that at the century mark in 2005, Sagamore Beach, still a community of summer families with more of them remaining year round, will be as fresh and healthy as our grandchildren who will then be the club's officers and governors. Their children in an unending circle will be The Bunch 'whose heart is young and whose life is as an eagle poised.'"

—Sydney Clark, *Sagamore Beach Colony, the First Fifty Years*

The Doran house, built in 1905, was the first house completed in the Sagamore Beach Colony. Built by George W. Stone, a lumber merchant, at first it housed many workers who constructed the other early houses. The house is still a summer cottage. Many of the bedrooms have private baths, built by the workers for their convenience. For many years, it was owned by the Sage family. In 1952, the cottage was purchased by George Doran from the Batchelders, Sage descendants. It is still owned by the Doran family, four generations of whom now live in the village. (Courtesy of David G. Curran.)

This 1992 aerial view of the former Sagamore Lodge lot shows new homes now on the property. (Courtesy of David G. Curran.)

Hon. Joseph Martin enjoyed living at the beach when he was not in Washington, D.C. His house is the one slightly to the right of center in the bend of the road.

The Sorentis were the first Italian family to settle on Cape Cod, in 1889. In 1989, 100 years later, Mr. and Mrs. Louis Sorenti celebrated their golden anniversary with their family in Sagamore. Seated are, from left to right, Marie Sorenti, Eleanor Regassi, Yolanda Sorenti, and Louis Sorenti. Standing are, from left to right, Ida Sorenti, Joseph Sorenti, Stella Ferretti, Frank Sorenti, and Dante "Pat" Sorenti.

A gathering of younger Sorenti generations includes, from left to right, Mary Joe, Janette, Michael, Joe, Mary, Jennifer, Judy, and Joe Jr. Seated are Jane and Jimmy.

Some members of the Doran clan are shown here at a reunion in July 1992, on the occasion of Dana Doran's christening. (Photograph by D. Curran.)

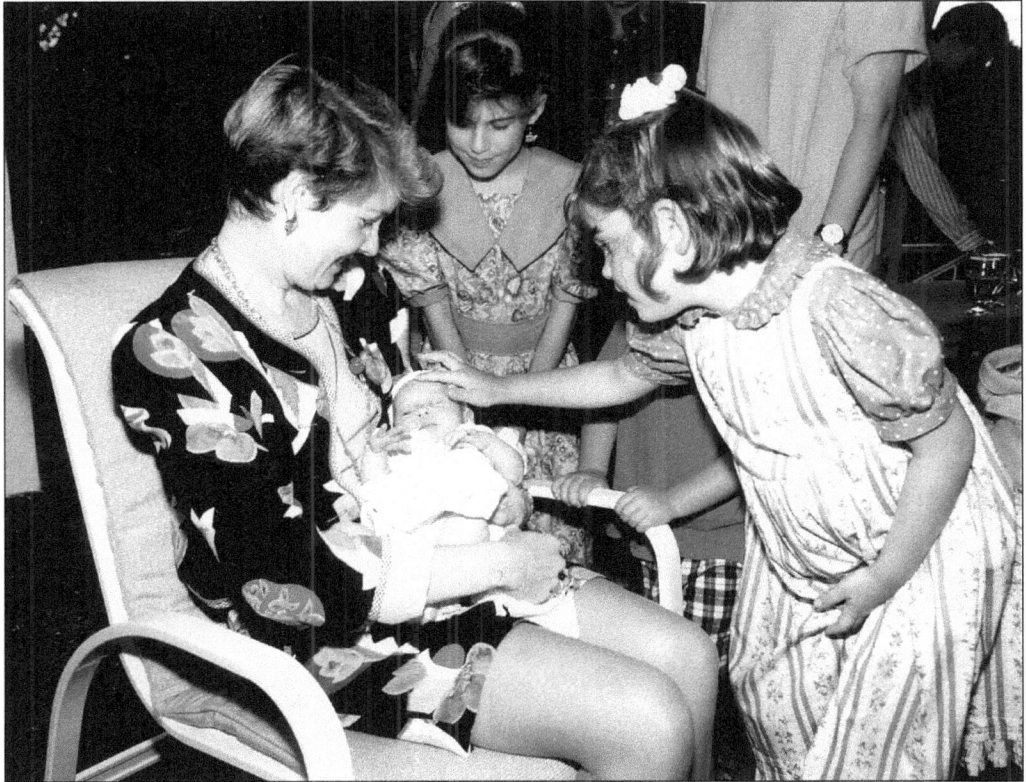

Dana Doran, the guest of honor at her christening, is in the arms of her mother, Susan Fisher Doran. Cousin Ali Doran is in the middle, and cousin Caitlyn Doran is to the right. (Photograph by D. Curran.)

These girls of summer are, from left to right, Ruth Anderson, Todd Reynolds, and Eleanor Doran.

Eleanor and George Doran are shown in 1992.

The musical Fagerburgs are gathered here. From left to right are the following: (front row) Rachel Fagerburg Menuel (with viola), Rudi Schipizky (with violin), Rachel Fagerburg, and Sara Nixon; (back row) Anne Fagerburg (with cello) and Karen Fagerburg (with violin). (Photograph by Stephen Begleiter.)

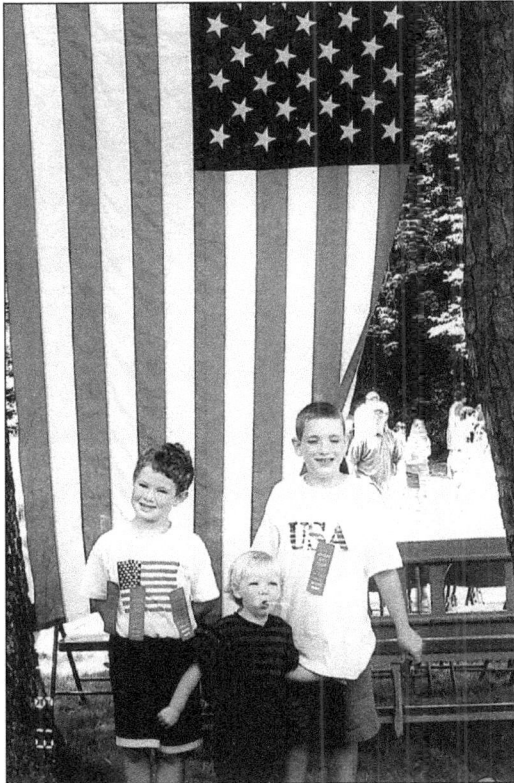

A patriotic fourth-generation family, the Donahue-Dolan clan includes, from left to right, Christopher McCahill, Brenden McCahill, and Patrick McCahill.

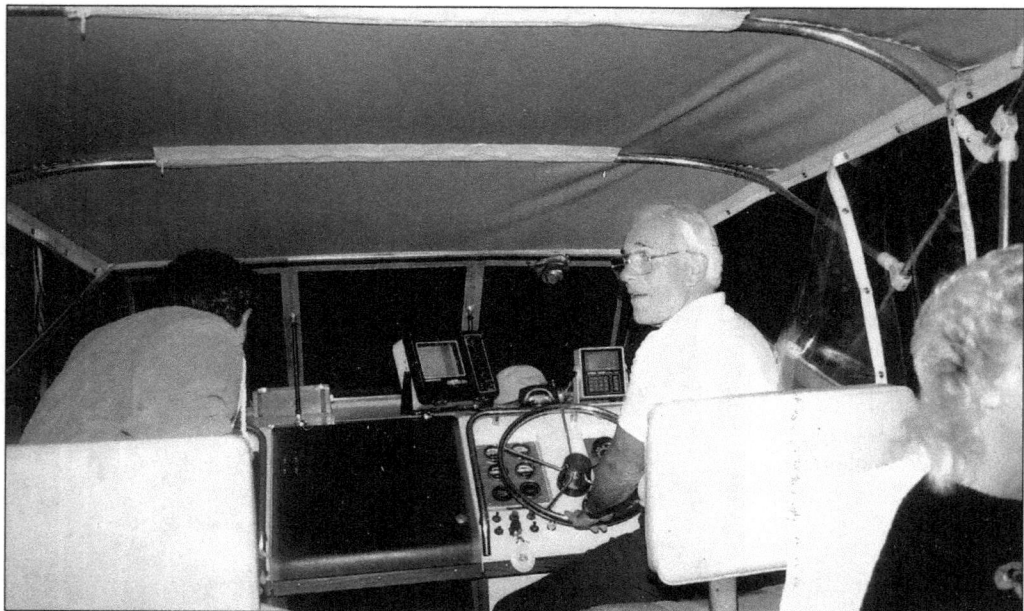

Russell Baker, at the helm, is taking his friends fishing.

Beverly and Heimar Niit came to Sagamore Beach in 1969, having bought the house formerly owned by the Holway family. They improved and expanded it as their family grew. Now their grandchildren also enjoy it.

The three friends here are, from left to right, Alex Rowley, Jessie Anderson, and Christa Niit.

This group at a summer party includes Susan Donovan Redman, JoAnn Murphy, Patty Tuohy Sharman, Joe Sharman, John Redman, and Bob Donovan.

Alan Werthen, president of the Sagamore Beach Colony Club in 1967–1968, is on stage in his favorite outfit.

Andrea Baker Rowley, past president of the Sagamore Beach Colony Club, and her husband, Andrew Rowley, are pictured here as newlyweds in the early 1970s.

Patty and Champe Fisher are shown on the Bluff at Sagamore Beach c. 1965.

Aboard the *Natalia* are, from left to right, Champe Fisher, Fred Fisher, and Clark Fisher.

Showing the patriotic spirit in 1944 are, from left to right, Lt. Henry Smith, Peggy Ann Donahue, and Eddie Dolan.

At the annual camp show, Jay Herlihy and Christa Niit present their team flag while other campers look on.

These junior team tennis winners are, from left to right, Scott Keery, Dan Buckley, Joe Harold, and Lars Niit.

The Thibault house, built in 1936, has an underground access from the beach. It was owned for many years by the Tennant family.

The Thibault house on Sagamore Road is shown as it looks today.

The Beekman cottage, at 105 Standish Road, is pictured c. 1920. It was bought furnished at auction in July 1929 by Frederick W. Hill for $2,350. The house had previously been used as a boardinghouse.

Now owned by Dr. Norman Hill, the family homestead is enjoyed by the fourth generation.

The Bonito house, a former garage, is located at 20 Sagamore Road.

The same scene today shows that the garage was converted c. 1960 to a waterfront home by Jack and Minette Baer.

This quiet scene on Hawes Road is usually filled with children (and an occasional dog) running between the Todd (left) and Fagerburg homes.

Windswept was built by the Pope family and used as a rental. (Courtesy of Norman Hill.)

Windswept, located on Williston Road, is now owned by Sally Baer, who summered here with her family in the 1950s and 1960s.

The Decaneas family of Wellesley purchased this home in 1949. Dr. Decaneas is pictured in front in the 1950s.

This house was owned by Dr. George Miller. It was one of the few winterized homes on the beach. The Millers were thus able to come off-season, because they had their own well.

The original Fisher house, built in 1933, is pictured here to the right. It is now the Donna Fisher house. To the left is the Davis house.

The Arnold homestead, on Williston Road, was painted by Edwina Eldridge.

This Zickell cottage at 84 Mayflower Road was owned by the Craig family in the 1930s, who rented it to the Wright family. The Gillis family owned it in the 1950s, passing it down to the Zickells of Boylston in the 1960s.

The Doran-Parry cottage was owned by the Tinkham family for many years and rented by the Lacey family. It was next owned by Joe and Bob Lane, who renovated it and sold it to the Parrys. George Doran Jr. and Nancy Parry Doran now reside here in summer with their children Allison, Courtney, Caitlyn, Jeff, and Chris.

In the 1930s, the Smith family owned this home. It was rented to Helen MacPherson for many years. One of Sagamore Beach's favorite political sons, Joseph Martin, lived here while he was Speaker of the House in Washington, D.C., in the 1950s. He passed it on to his niece Ginny Doyle in 1977. (Courtesy of Bourne Historical Society and Archives.)

The St. Yves house, at 226 Standish Road, was owned by Frank and Mabel Batchelder of Worcester for many years. Their son Joe married Ebby Sage and lived there as well. The O'Keefe family owned it in the 1970s and 1980s. It is now owned by the St. Yves family, formerly of Taunton.

The Leveroni house, at 412 Williston Road, was formerly owned by Mrs. Dunlop and her grandchildren, the Hicklers, in the 1930s.

The Herlihy house was built by Sam Twombly in 1906. It was later owned by Chester Pratt, the neighborhood handyman for many years. The Herlihys now own it, and many children and grandchildren fill it in summer.

One of the colony's first homes is this Leis house, built *c.* 1910. First owned by the DeWitt True family and then by the Adams family, it was passed down through the generations to Polly and Joe Leis.

Owned by the Mullin family for many years, this house was home to Jim, Julia, and Margaret Mullin of Needham year-round. They looked after the neighborhood when the summer people left. Then Christine, Gary, Maggie, and Joe Todd of Wellesley renovated the house, and they now come with their dog Daisy each summer.

This *c.* 1930 view from the piazza of Norman Hill's house shows the Bradford Arms, the Arnold house, the Gleason cottage, the Hildreth cottage (now owned by the Kerrys), and the Dawes cottage.

These homes are pictured back when Sagamore Road was just dirt. From left to right are the Stanton house, the Fagerburg and Todd house, and the Congdon and Ryan houses (foreground).

The Tuohy house is located on Phillips Road.

The Tinkham cottage (*c.* 1938), on Hawes Road, is now owned by the Parry-Doran family. (Courtesy of Rachel Fagerburg.)

This is an aerial view of some of the cottages along the beach. (Courtesy of David Curran.)

Left: An excellent example of the generations in Sagamore Beach is the Fisher family. Pictured here is Frederick G. Fisher Sr., president of the Sagamore Beach Colony Club in 1954–1956. *Right:* Frederick G. Fisher Jr. was president of the club in 1964–1965. A senior partner at the law firm of Hale and Dorr in Boston, he retired to Sagamore Beach and renovated the family home, just before his untimely death in Tel Aviv in 1989. His widow, Talia Bebz Fisher, has opened the home for garden tours.

Clark W. Fisher, president of the Sagamore Beach Colony Club in 1996–1997 and brother of Frederick Jr., carries on the family traditions. Another brother, Champe Fisher, pictured on page 107, is also a past president of the Sagamore Beach Colony Club.

Harold Clark Hall, the former Assembly Hall, was renamed in honor of the faithful treasurer for many years. Clark was a son of the colony's founder, Rev. Dr. Frances E. Clark, another reminder of the generations continuing at Sagamore Beach Colony.

The Little Store, one of the anchors of the community, is pictured here in 2002.

SAGAMORE BEACH COLONY CLUB PRESIDENTS

1910–1912	Dr. Edward S. Hawes	1958–1959	Arno Erkkila
1913	Mrs. Frank Tinkham	1960	Russell McDonnell
1914	Dr. George Coleman	1961	Walter Ryan
1915	Dr. Francis E. Clark	1962–1963	Rita MacDonald
1916–1917	Mrs. Arthur J. Crockett	1964–1965	Frederick Fisher Jr.
1918	Mrs. George W. Coleman	1966	Richard Holway
1919–1920	Frank L. Tinkham	1967–1968	Alan Werthen
1921–1923	J.J. Hyland	1969–1970	Arthur LaCroix
1924–1925	Mrs. Frank R. Batchelder	1971–1972	Thomas Keery
1926–1927	Mrs. Henry C. Fuller	1973	Leo Kelly
1928–1929	Mrs. Sydney J. True	1974–1975	Donald Doyle
1930	Mrs. Merton Sage	1976–1977	Heimer Niit
1931–1932	Mrs. Chester L. Witaker	1978	Champe Fisher
1933–1934	Edward S. Alden	1979–1980	Joe Harold
1935–1936	Alexander B. Campbell	1981–1982	James Queenan
1937–1938	Laura Ludin	1983–1984	Robert L. Tennant
1939–1940	David J. White	1985–1986	Charles Kiklis
1941–1942	Theron Batchelder	1987	Robert Buckley
1943–1945	Herbert P. Arnold	1988–1989	Angelo Borelli
1946–1947	A. Wellesley Hannington	1990–1991	Robert Parry
1948–1950	Harold S. Clark	1992–1993	Andrea Rowley
1951	T. Edmund Garrity	1994–1995	Joseph C. Sharman
1952	Edward M. Hawes	1996–1997	Clark Fisher
1953	John D. Neill	1998–1999	John Redman
1954–1956	Frederick G. Fisher	2000–2001	James E. Sullivan
1957	John Baer	2002–2003	Andy Anderson

THE FIRST COTTAGE OWNERS OF SAGAMORE BEACH

Adams, Rev. and Mrs. Harry C.,
71 Williston Road.

Baker, Dr. and Mrs. George T.,
96 Shawmut Road.

Bades, Marion B., 100 Cautaumet Road.

Beekman, Mathena, 202 Standish Road
(Dr. Norman Hill).

Birchard, Florence W., 107 Sagamore Road.

Cathcart, Rev. and Mrs. S.M., 9 Williston
Road (Pappas, Smith).

Clark, Rev. and Mrs. Francis E., 118
Sagamore Road (John Doran).

Coleman, Mr. and Mrs. George W., 147
Sagamore Road (Frizell, Clapp, Adams).

Cook, Alice R., 5 Clark Road (F. Boles).

Crane, Francis P., 130 Cohasset Road.

Donovan, Mr. and Mrs. James 356 Standish
Road (Batchelder, O'Keefe, St. Yves).

Dunlop, Rev. and Mrs. J.J., 142 Cohasset
Road (Durgin, Massard).

Ellis, Mr. and Mrs. C.G., 92 Shawmut Road.

Ellis, Mr. and Mrs. E.R., 15 Massasoit Road.

Mr. and Mrs. Albert Wood, 348 Phillips
Road.

Graff, Mr. and Mrs. George B., 144 Sagamore
Road (Paliuca, Morgan).

Hawes, Mr. Edward S., and the Misses Hawes
128 Cohasset Road.

Hinds, Mr. and Mrs. W.H., 138 Clark Road
(Howard, Baker).

Jackson, Mr. and Mrs. Willard W., 392
Phillips Road.

Kneeland, Rev. and Mrs. M.D., 101
Shawmut Road (Young, Tucker).

Knight, Edward F., 435 Phillips Road.

Lathrup, Mr. and Mrs. H.N., 146 Sagamore
Road (Green, Adams).

Merrick, Rev. and Mrs. Frank W.,
88 Pocasset Road (Farnum).

Merrick, Rev. and Mrs. Frank W., 233
Williston Road.

Nickerson, Mr. and Mrs. S.L., 125 Sagamore
Road (Martin Putnam).

Page, Martha F., 102 Shawmut Road.

Phillips, Rev. and Mrs. E.E.,
433 Phillips Road.

Richardson, H.T., 94 Shawmut Road.

Schuerch, Mr. and Mrs. E.W., 78 Megansett
Road (Fuller).

Shaw, Mr. and Mrs. William, 145 Sagamore
Road, (Baer, Erkkila, Lane).

Smith, Elma, 93 Shawmut Road.
(Hannington, Sherman, Freed).

Stone, Mr. and Mrs. R.B., 367 Phillips Road.

Thayer, Mr. and Mrs. C.A., 164 Robinson
Road (Donahue, Dolan).

Tinkham, Mr. and Mrs. Frank L.,
132 Cohasset Road (Campbell, Lane,
Parry, Doran).

Tirrell, Rev. and Mrs. Eben,
125 Sagamore Road.

Upham, Henry, 139 Sagamore Road.

Warner, Henrietta C., 235 Priscilla Road
(Walter Green).

Webber, Dr. and Mrs. Samuel G., 123
Sagamore Road (Allen).

Wells, Prof. and Mrs. Amos R.E., 121
Sagamore Road (A.H. Clark).

White, Rev. and Mrs. Eliot, 122 Sagamore
Road (Sage, George Doran).

Whiting, Rev. and Mrs. Elbridge C.,
99 Cautaumet Road.

Williams, Mr. and Mrs. George B.,
108 Sagamore Road.

Wolcott, Rev. William E., 158 Williston
Road (Jacobi).

Woods, Ida E., 126 Samoset Road
(Skelton, Roffe).

BIBLIOGRAPHY

Bonfanti, Leo. *Biographies and Legends of New England Indians*. Wakefield, Massachusetts: Pride Publications, 1969.

Butler, Gerald. *The Military History of Cape Cod*. Charleston, South Carolina: Arcadia Publishing, 2002.

Clark, Don, Dottie Clark, Muriel and Henry Pappas, and Frannie Tidemarsh. *The 75th Anniversary of the Sagamore Beach Colony Club 1905–1980*. Boston: Sagamore Beach Colony Club, 1980.

Clark, Sydney. *Sagamore Beach Colony, the First Fifty Years 1905–1985*. Boston: Sagamore Beach Colony Club, 1955.

Deyo, Simeon L. *History of Barnstable County: 1620–1890*. New York: H.W. Blake, 1890.

Gould, James. *First Settlers of Sandwich, West Side*. Cape Cod Genealogical Society Journal, spring-summer 1997.

Lovell, Russell A., Jr. *Sandwich: A Cape Cod Town*. Sandwich, Massachusetts: Town of Sandwich Archives and Historical Center, 1986.

Vuilleumier, Marion. *Indians on Olde Cape Cod*. Taunton, Massachusetts: William S. Sullwold Publishing, 1970.

———. *Sandwich: Cape Cod's Oldest Town*. Charleston, South Carolina: Arcadia Publishing, 2002.

www.ingramcontent.com/pod-product-compliance
Lightning Source LLC
Chambersburg PA
CBHW050548110426
42813CB00008B/2292